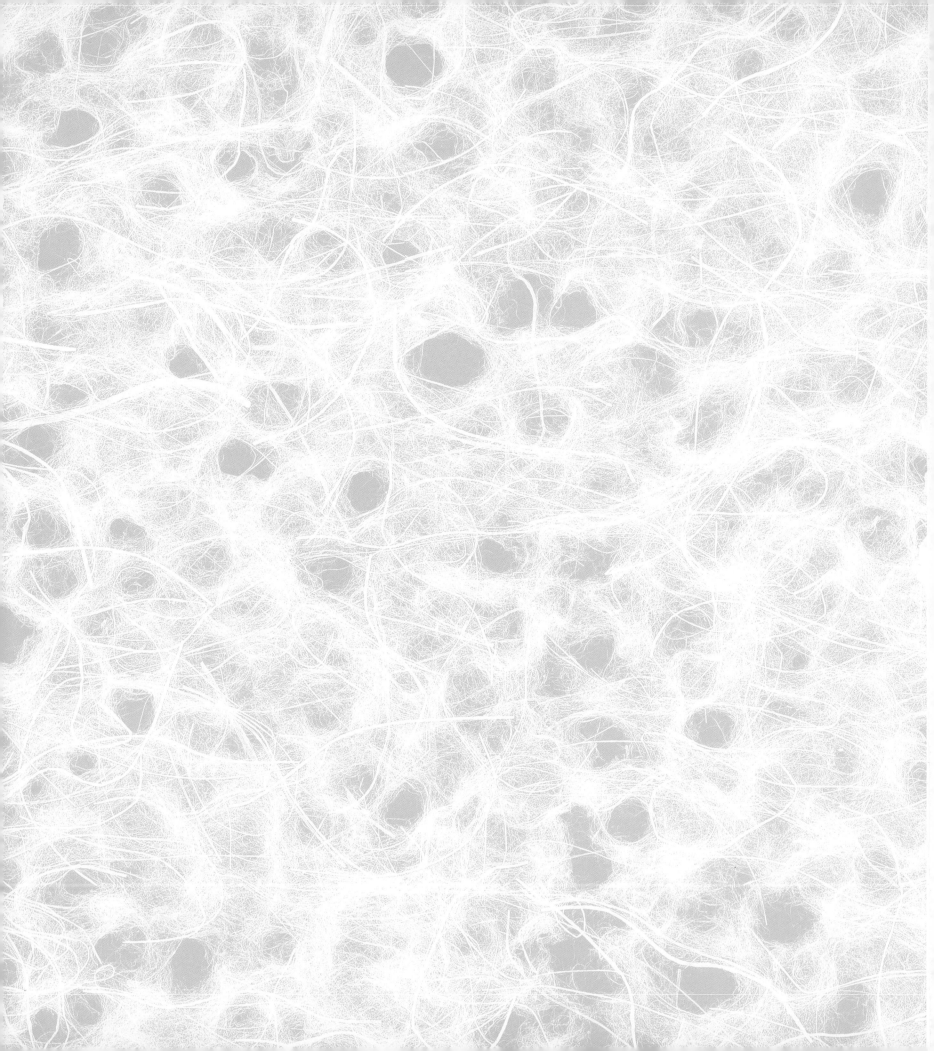

Witches

LORI EISENKRAFT-PALAZZOLA

Witches

A BOOK OF MAGIC AND WISDOM

SMITHMARK

Witches
A BOOK OF MAGIC AND WISDOM

This edition published in 1999 by SMITHMARK Publishers,
a division of U.S. Media Holdings, Inc.,
115 West 18th Street, New York, NY 10011.

Project Director: Elizabeth Viscott Sullivan
Editor: Jean Mills
Concept & Idea: Janine Weitenauer
Design Team of 360 Degrees:
Anya Lemkova, Devorah Wolf,
Herta Kriegner, Shahira Youssef
Art Research: Anita Dickhuth

SMITHMARK books are available for bulk purchase
for sales promotion and premium use.
For details write or call the manager of special sales,
SMITHMARK Publishers,
115 West 18th Street, New York, NY 10011; 212-519-1300

ISBN: 0-7651-1058-X
Printed in Hong Kong
10 9 8 7 6 5 4 3 2 1
Library of congress CIP

Eisenkraft-Palazzola, Lori.
    Witches : a book of magic and wisdom / Lori
Eisenkraft-Palazzola.
        p. cm.
    Includes bibliographical references and index.
    ISNB 0-7651-1058-x (alk. paper)
    1. Witchcraft—History. 2. Witches—History. I. Title.
133.4'3'09—dc21
                                        98-4524
                                        CIP

This book is intended as an entertaining historical reference only.
Any literal usage of the contents of this book is the sole responsibility of the reader.

*For **Dora** and **Sam** Eichenthal*
and
***Murray** and **Mary** Eisenkraft*

I wish you were here to see this,
But I think you know anyway...

Acknowledgments

*Profuse appreciation and gratitude go out to my mother, **Lenore Eisenkraft,** brother, **Gary Eisenkraft,***
*and **Steve B.** for all their help, patience—and especially for customized Tech Support!*

*Many thanks to my husband, **Richard,** for his support, enthusiasm, and lower-volume shouting*
at the New York Yankees and Mets (and thank-you to the Yankees for winning the World Series !),
while I told him every day for six months "I can't, now—I'm busy with Witches and Faeries!"

I am especially grateful for all of those—family and friends, neighbors and
co-workers—who showed great confidence and enthusiasm in my books.

*Special thanks to **Janine Weitenauer,** who radiates a true spark of magic, and whose idea all of this was in the first place;*
***Anya Lemkova** and **Devorah Wolf,** both of whose design expertise totally blew me away; and **Anya,** again, for her "dead hand"*
*and other bizarre and wonderful ideas; my editor, **Jean Mills,** who directed me down the proper path when I languished too long*
*at the crossroads; **Nicole A. Rénaud,** for her sweet nature, helpfulness, and calm—every company needs a Nicole;*
***Margaux King,** who, even in 1980, I knew there was something magical about—and it still hits me every time we meet;*
*and **Anita Dickhuth,** who patiently let me whine and moan about woodcuts and "perfect pictures."*

TABLE OF CONTENTS

But if
knowled
desired
accursed
" You

the
stand
d !"

A Concise History of Witches

arriors and knights fell in love with them. Gods, heroes, and kings consorted with them. They were powerful queens, warrior goddesses, glamorous enchantresses, and sorceresses extraordinaire. They were witches. And their world was a realm of beauty, eroticism, nature, and enchantment.

Witches have existed for thousands of years. In fact, the practice of witchcraft stretches far beyond recorded history. Archaeologists have found cave paintings in various places, such as Lascaux in the south of France, rock paintings in the Sahara, and have come upon a number of of Paleolithic drawings, all of which scholars believe had magical meaning for prehistoric people. But no one is quite sure who any of those prehistoric people were. The painting in Lascaux, for example, dates back some 25,000 years. Known as the Dead Man, it seems to depict a dead warrior, or a shaman in a meditative trance. Its location is hard to find and difficult to reach, because one must descend a shaft to see it. General belief is that, since the ancient Celtic tribes buried their people in shafts or pits, and their Druid priests tossed offerings and sacrificial items down shafts, it seems likely the painting has Celtic ties. And the excavated grave of a Bronze Age woman in Hallstatt, near Salzburg, Austria, has yielded objects that are considered even today to be magical or shamanistic. Again, evidence leads scholars and archaeologists to the ancient Celts, a mighty warrior people whose heyday occurred throughout a great deal of the Bronze Age and on into the Iron Age. And it is the Celtic people from whom we've inherited a great deal of our history, legends, and myths about witches.

Little ancient Celtic history exists in written form, because the Celts taught their children by example, and passed on history and their experiences by means of storytelling. Led by a Druid bard (poet, storyteller, and magician), with family members and elders adding to the tale, the Celts were quite fond of storytelling, embellishing and exaggerating all the way, creating lively and colorful accounts of their history, entwined with myth and legend. What *is* their "real" truth?

We do know that magic and communing with nature were the Celts' way of life. Many of them, but not all, possessed a different degree of magical power, and the Druids were the most powerful of all. Often, an individual was identified with the aspect of nature she or he was able to work with best. For example, the element of Fire could be summoned by one person to light the hearth, without having to use flint, while another person had a grasp on the element of Earth, from which she could glean healing properties. These people drew out and pulled within themselves the energies of nature.

Epona's element was Earth. A beautiful young Celt from Gaul, she was the goddess of horses, and the word "pony" is derived from her name. Epona possessed much knowledge and magic and was said to be the daughter of a Druid and a mare. Horses being of utmost importance to the equestrian Celts, she was regarded as a very powerful deity who was able to meld with and heal horses, and shape-shift into a mare. Epona's popularity surged in ancient Rome, where it grew to cult proportions. The Roman army had brought word of her to the Empire, and awe of the mare goddess spread like wildfire. The only Celtic goddess ever worshiped in Rome, legions celebrated her as the goddess who watched over their horses, while other worshipers carved mares on chalky hills and dressed as horses at feasts in her honor. Also known as a river goddess and fertility goddess, Epona seems to share her horse identity with Rhiannon.

Rhiannon was the Welsh moon goddess of the Cymry (meaning "friends" in Gaelic), and is also known as the goddess of the Underworld, goddess of joy and oblivion, queen of night, queen of Hell, and an enchantress. Her name comes from an ancient fertility mother called Rigantona, meaning "great queen." Rhiannon's story is the oldest one found in a collection of ancient Welsh tales today known as *The Mabinogion.* Her ties to Epona are illustrated not only by the incredibly fast and tireless horse she rode, her glossy long hair flying like streamers behind her, but also in the punishment she received when falsely accused of murdering and eating her newborn son. Dressed in a gold-trimmed clingy white gown, and astride her swift horse, the ethereal beauty Rhiannon flew as quick as the wind, always accompanied by magical birds. The birds, who were said to be able to wake the dead and put the living to sleep for seven years, were likely this witch's familiars. She gave birth to a son on Beltane Day, and he was kidnapped from the palace she shared with her husband that night while they slept. Rhiannon was found the next morning with blood on her face and puppy bones scattered about her. She had been framed. For "devouring" her baby she was sentenced to greet visitors at the gate outside the palace by telling them of her crime. She then had to walk on all fours while carrying guests on her back as though she were a horse. This relates to one of Rhiannon's identities as an earth goddess as well as a goddess of mares. Eventually a peasant who had found her son returned him, and Rhiannon was absolved of any wrongdoing. Later legends portrayed her both as a muse and the Arthurian Lady of the Lake, and it is believed that she is a descendant of Epona.

Much of ancient Celtic history regarding witchcraft and the magical arts is lost to us, appearing in disjointed form in several sources, and even then, the few short paragraphs are nearly identical except for some minor additions or slight differences in interpretation. The Celts themselves left no written records until sometime after 1000 C.E.—probably after the Norman Conquest of 1066. There is much information on Celtic history in general, but to learn about witchcraft and magic, we need to turn to the most extensive documentation that can be found. This is a book of ancient Welsh stories, called *The Mabinogion*. Originally scribed by different writers in different centuries (c. 1100–1300 B.C.E.), these tales were gathered together and published in a compilation by Lady Charlotte Guest during the years 1938–1949. Once passed down through generations orally, the stories are often confusing and muddled, because missing information has left great gaps. This is likely the result of events being documented so many years after they actually took place; bits and pieces of history would have been lost or forgotten over hundreds—even thousands—of years, after all, and the writers themselves had probably heard variations of the tales as well. But scholars have taken much effort in making sense of and explaining

these historical accounts. And it is in *The Mabinogion*, the writing perhaps begun by the Druids themselves, that we find our information on the great Celtic witches such as Cerridwen, Rhiannon, and the Morrigán. It is a book of gods, goddesses, and kings; warriors, heroes, and heroines; magic, sorcery, and witchcraft; and good and evil.

Horses being of utmost importance to the equestrian Celts, Epona was regarded as a very powerful deity who was able to meld with and heal horses, and shape-shift into a mare.

The Morrigán was the most famous Celtic war goddess as well as a goddess of death. She was a seductress who had many lovers, and would retaliate against those who spurned her. She had long, blazing red hair, could shape-shift into a raven or a snake, was said to be a giant when she took on her human identity, and was a Triple Goddess of ancient Ireland. The Morrigán would wing through the sky in her raven form, warning of coming battle. She was known to cast runes and chant magical charms to divine the victors of war, and she invoked spells to protect her favorite warriors. It was said that the Morrigán flew across battlefields screeching her wild cry of encourage-ment to the spirits of the slain, but it was also believed that she was in search of fresh meat! The Morrigán had a collection of severed heads that she treasured, for it was believed that the heads of slain great warriors yielded much magical power. As Morgan le Fay ("le fay" means "the fairy") of Arthurian legend, she was said to be Merlin the Magician's underhanded lover and also the queen of Avalon, or the Land of Apples, where Excalibur was forged. Avalon was an Otherworld where partaking of the magical apples gave one immortality. It is believed that Morgan herself carried the wounded King Arthur, who may have been her brother or half-brother, to Avalon, healed him, and that they live there still.

Cerridwen was a Welsh goddess of the Cymri. Her symbol is the cauldron, and she was a deity of grain and nature, fertility, and poetic inspiration. Her identity had three facets: she was known as the hag of darkness and rebirth, warrior maiden, and earth mother. She was also an enchantress and a shape-shifter who would turn into a vicious kitten, or a white pig that sometimes went about the country giving out gifts of grain and honeybees. Cerridwen lived with her husband and children on an island in the middle of a lake. Her daughter, Creirwy, was known as the most beautiful little girl in the world, and her son, Avagduu, the ugliest boy. To help make up for her son's unfortunate lack of appeal, Cerridwen mixed a magical potion that was to give her son knowledge and inspiration. She brewed the mixture in her cauldron for a year. One day while she was out gathering herbs, the mortal Gwion, whom she'd left to tend the cauldron, unfortunately managed to ingest a few drops, which had splashed on his finger. Gwion fled, and Cerridwen, enraged that a human had gained the powers intended for her son, went after him. Gwion shape shifted alternately into a hare, a fish, a bird, and a grain of wheat. Cerridwen in turn shape-shifted in pursuit turning herself into a greyhound, an otter, a hawk, and finally a hen who ate Gwion as a grain. Nine months later she birthed him as a son, and cast him into the sea. A prince rescued the baby and named him Taliesin, and he later grew up to become a bard of great renown

12

...she was said to be Merlin the Magician's underhanded lover and also the queen of Avalon...

13

Brigid was a goddess of fire and her name means "bright one" in Gaelic. Eventually "adopted" by the Christians, she was the daughter of a Druid and a Triple Goddess of the Irish. Unlike other triple deities who morphed through three different identities as maiden, mother, and crone, Brigid's facets were three different aspects of the same deity. One of the most celebrated of all Celtic goddesses, Brigid, or Brigantia (in Gaelic, High One), was the goddess of smithing, ruler of inspiration and poetry, for which she carried a cauldron, and goddess of healing. Scholars suggest that Brigid's history extends beyond the Celts, perhaps back to another ancient race of people called the Tuatha dé Danann. The Tuatha dé Danann inhabited Ireland before the Celts, and Eire is named for one of their goddess-queens. It is believed that the Celts gleaned a number of their goddesses from this ancient warrior tribe. Brigid was such a popular goddess to the pagans that the Christians canonized her, and she became known as St. Bridget.

Of course, the Celts were not the only culture to have the benefit of witches. In ancient Greece, in the ninth century, the poet Homer included in his tale the *Odyssey*, a stunningly beautiful witch, or sorceress, named Circe. Unfortunately not a kindly sort, Circe was a moon goddess who is best known for changing men into wolves, lions, and swine. Said to be the daughter of Perse, a cunning sea nymph who practiced black magic, and the sun god Helios, she was also known as the daughter of Hecate, Greek goddess of the Underworld, patron and overseer of magic and witchcraft, and protector of all witches.

Circe was accused of murdering her husband, either because she resented the dishonor of being merely dismissed as part of his harem or because she desired to rule the land herself. Rather than see her be stoned to death for her crime, her father swiftly came to her rescue and spirited her away to an island she could rule as her own. There, the enchantress whiled away the days mixing magical potions, weaving at her loom, singing beautiful songs, dining and having sex with her visitors, and turning her guests into animals—most notably, pigs.

Hecate was another ancient Greek goddess, although scholars argue that her true origin was Thracian. Multifaceted, she was a moon goddess, fertility goddess, and queen of night. She had power on land, sea, and in the sky, and was often seen by humans riding her moon chariot. Hecate was a Triple Goddess, as well, meaning she bore three identities: maiden, mother, and crone. Hecate had three heads: according to some lore, these were a horse, a dog, and a serpent. A variation was that she possessed the heads of a dog, a lion, and a mare atop a serpent's body. At any rate, Hecate could look three ways at one time.

This likely accounts for her role as the goddess of crossroads—a place where anyone could look in three directions at the same time. Those who worshiped her erected statues (which still exist to this day) in her likeness at those sites, held ceremonies of great magic there, and left her offerings of milk, honey, and corn. Also known as the supervisor of all magical arts, goddess of black magic, and the queen of the spirits of the dead, the queen of night would sometimes wander about near midnight with a pack of red-eyed hellhounds and dead souls, gathering the gifts left in her honor. The Greeks believed Hecate could give to and take from humankind anything she wished. And perhaps she did: she was known to grant those who celebrated her with keen hunting skill, victorious battles, great powers, and wealth.

Many of us know Hecate by another name: Diana, Roman goddess of the hunt as well as moon goddess and goddess of the Underworld, and protectress of wild animals. Diana is also one of the Triple Goddesses of modern witchcraft, along with Selene, shape-shifter and winged Greek goddess of the moon, and Hecate. As a Triple Goddess, Diana's statues sometimes had three heads: a lion, a dog, and a boar—erected, of course, at sites where three roads met.

Artemis was Diana's Greek counterpart. She was the virgin goddess of childbirth and protector of innocence, children, and baby animals. Artemis hunted with silver arrows and a pack of immortal dogs, sometimes chasing after her prey in a silver moon chariot. Only a minor goddess to the Greeks, the immortal beauty punished humans for such crimes as shooting the deer that she herself hunted, and basically terrorized those who crossed her.

In the Roman Empire, when sorcery was fashionable, the wealthy paid for a glimpse into the future: magicians were lively entertainment. The Romans did not see white (good) magic as a threat. However, black (evil) magic was treated as a civil crime, and a supernatural threat to the emperor or state was a fate punishable by torture and death.

In ancient times, the practice of witchcraft, sorcery, and magic was a way of life for many cultures; no one questioned the aid of a diviner or healer. But things changed. As humanity evolved and Christianity spread, the old ways were forced to take a backseat. Fear of anything "pagan" threw Christians into an uproar, and they used any means necessary to eliminate religions that were not their own. And witches of any sort, even healers or wise women, were dealt a bad hand.

The early Christians viewed the Pagan religion and its traditions as the ultimate insult, and their solution to the problem of resistant converts was punishment both swift and harsh. Strange beliefs and terror regarding witches sprouted with the rabid Christians, as they sought a way to claim ancient cultures by force. Chaos reigned as the Pagans fought back, culminating with a great clash of war, torturous retribution, and death. The toll was so great, even the Pagans recoiled in horror. In an effort to circumvent constant battle, the Christians decided that a good way to convert people was to equate all things pagan—magic and witchcraft, beliefs and legends, festivals and rituals, and gods and goddesses—with evil, and especially the devil.

Most religions placed women on the bottom rung of the ladder. Their feelings, ideas, and contributions were stifled by the male-dominated world, and often, women were outright shunned. They were not allowed to enter temples of worship, and in some cultures, not even permitted to dine with their husbands. As Christianity sought to conquer and enmesh such varied peoples, who were steeped in their own superstitions, deities, and customs—never mind that the Christians had their own strange beliefs—it was likely that some women revolted on their own behalf. They had no political or social strength, and thus were easy targets for the long arm of a crushing Christianity. And the actions of these heroic women during a period of great unrest led to unfortunate results, with the cry of heresy first among them. Soon, the beautiful, immortal witch- goddesses had became a vague memory of times long gone.

The low social standing of women set the stage for the havoc that was to be wreaked for many hundreds of years to come. As Christianity toppled the gods and goddesses, along with magic and the worship of nature (though they were forced to integrate certain celebrations, rituals, and deities that are still honored today), daily life was rife with mysterious events and undefinable occurrences. Where did such unexplainable diseases and afflictions as plague, deformities, and madness come from? What caused blighted crops and ailing cattle, changes in weather and astronomical wonders, and the death of newborns? Witches and the devil, of course, according to overzealous Christian fanatics. And to make matters worse, these unfortunate conditions were decreed as punishment for nonbelievers in the Christian Lord and retribution for rejection of the Christian faith.

The people were now frightened. Magic had become the epitome of evil. We know today that the devil was an invention of early Christians, formulated to scare the hell out of people. (Note that they used Hel, Scandinavian goddess and queen of the Underworld, to name their place of eternal punishment.) Witches, healers, seers, sorcerers, and magicians became the enemy. Celebrations of nature, worship of ancient gods and goddesses and heroes and kings, peering into the future, and practice of the healing arts were forced underground.

In ancient times, the practice of witchcraft, sorcery, and magic was a way of life for many cultures; no one questioned the aid of a diviner or healer.

The first "heretic" was burned to death in France in 1022. Stories about witches from so-called first- and secondhand accounts became rampant beginning in the twelfth century. The witch hysteria of the Middle Ages had begun. Logical thought was the exception, not the rule, in those days. The Church played upon simple peoples' ignorance and fright, and any lapses in "God-fearing" behaviors were dealt with severely, for the Church sought to make examples of the disobedient and non- or reluctant believers. The witch frenzy that was now spreading rapidly was purely a product of warped minds, overzealous, overly devout, or incredibly ignorant, twisted and cruel people. It was an abominable creation of bizarre proportions that would bear enormous repercussions.

Much of what we know about witch-hunts comes to us from a history spanning the 1400s through the 1700s. Mass hysteria commanded ordinary citizens—especially women, but also men and children—to be burned at the stake. Accusations of hateful or jealous neighbors caused the drowning of innocent victims, and plain old maliciousness of those who *swore* they saw a woman *flying on a broomstick* resulted in courtroom mockery and heinous deaths. And the Inquisition, begun in 1233, had added even more fuel to the fire.

The terrors of the papal Inquisition in the Middle Ages were unleashed on many victims. Witches, magicians, conjurors, and non-Christians suffered blame and punishment for a variety of absurd accusations. Seen as public enemies during a time of religious, social, and political chaos, these people were interrogated and tortured, tried and punished, and sometimes—not always—sentenced to death.

Carried out in Europe from the thirteenth through the fifteenth century, this madness was responsible for yet more needless deaths. Witch-hunts continued worldwide through the eighteenth century.

Many of us are familiar with the Salem witch trials and the hysteria with which they were associated. As abominable as they seem today, they were a small-scale version of the widespread persecution and countless burnings, tortures, and murders committed throughout Europe—all in the name of God. For example, the witches of Salem were hanged. A small mercy, for many of those in Europe were burned. It was believed that burning a witch was the only way to release the evil, as the devil would be forced to exit the melting body through the smoke.

It became "common knowledge" that unnatural abilities were evil. In other words, if you had more skill or knowledge than the woman next to you, then you must have sold your soul to the devil to gain such powers. It was said that witches were ugly hags who turned their neighbors into animals, spoiled milk, concocted poisons, made themselves invisible with an ointment they mixed for such terrible purposes, and wreaked havoc on the community. Why, everyone knew that witches left their homes in the dark of night, while normal people slept, and flew on a broomstick with their cat familiars to gather at the appointed hour—midnight: the Witching Hour. It was said that they convened in a cave, a clearing in the woods, or a grotto, to hold their Witches Sabbath. This would likely include a child sacrifice, some levitation, a drink or two of blood, feasting and consorting with imps and demons, a visit from Satan himself, and then the traditional orgy. After the party, the witches sneaked home without waking a soul and crept back into bed, with no one the wiser.

...more than 100,000 innocent people were murdered over a period of hundreds of years due to a basic human fear of the unknown.

Now, the very same people who spread such rumors, hypocrites that they were, would make their way in dark of night to a witch's home, begging an elixir for an ailing spouse, a decoction or powder for a weakened heart, or a draught for a sickly child. They came for amulets, spells, and charms; they begged for love potions and herbs, fortune-telling and healing. And the slandered witch did not send them away, but instead, used whatever healing aids were available—herbs, ointments, and teas, plants, roots, and salves—to cure. Oftentimes these treatments helped, but if the witch's skills and knowledge failed to produce the desired results, and especially if death overcame the patient, vicious assault soon followed as a thank-you for her gracious assistance: "You murdered my child!" "Spawn of Satan, you blinked at my mother last week, and now she's blind!" "The witch blighted my herd!" "She brought drought to our village! She dances with the devil!" "Burn the witch! Burn her!"

Yet, as eagerly sought as she was shunned, the everyday witch was *not* evil. She simply made potions and cures, practiced magic and spell-casting, and communed with the natural world. She was merely "different." And sadly, that difference led to her persecution as scapegoat for any malady that occurred in the community. Unfortunately, along with the witch, all people who practiced the magical arts, such as wizards, magicians, conjurors, seers, and others, eventually fell out of fashion and

Being an Account of the

TRYALS

OF

Several Witches,

Lately Excuted in

NEW-ENGLAND:

And of feveral remarkable. Curtofities therein Occurring.

Together with,

I. Obfervations upon the Nature, the Number, and the Operations of the Devils.

II. A fhort Narrative of a late outrage committed by a knot of Witches in *Swede-Land*, very much refembling, and fo far explaining, that under which *New-England* has laboured.

III. Some Councels directing a due Improvement of the Terrible things lately done by the unufual and amazing Range of *Evil-Spirits* in *New-England*.

IV. A brief Difcourfe upon thofe *Temptations* which are the more ordinary Devices of Satan.

By *COTTON MATHER.*

Publifhed by the Special Command of his EXCELLENCY the Goverreur of the Province of the *Maffachufetts-Bay* in *New-England.*

Printed firft, at *Boftun* in *New-England*; and Reprinted at *London*, for *John Dunton*, at the *Raven* in the *Pudtey*. 1693.

began to be regarded with suspicion as well. Soon, they too, were persecuted and forced underground, taking their magic and secrets with them.

Today, much of what we now about witches is for the most part fictional. Books and movies such as *The Wizard of Oz, Bedknobs and Broomsticks,* the devil-centered *Witches of Eastwick,* and the box-office dud *The Craft,* relied heavily on fantasy, misconception, thriller tactics, and, sometimes, just a bit of reality. Halloween witches with pointy hats and warty faces, flying on broomsticks with their black cats or owls perched at the end are living dinosaurs of another era. There were likely no such occurrences as Black Masses and prayers recited backwards; there were no hags dressed in black flying through the darkness astride wild boars, nor sacrificial children spirited away in the darkest hours; there were no levitations or drunken orgies with the devil or demons. What is true is that more than 100,000 innocent people were murdered over a period of hundreds of years due to a basic human fear of the unknown.

And so, if you should gaze up at the sky one inky-blue evening and catch sight of a goddess-witch breezing across the night sky in her moon chariot, long hair flying like ribbons in her wake, don't give in to the past and hide your eyes in fear. Honor her instead with a small nod of acknowledgment, a wink, and a smile, and she will look on you kindly for evermore.

*T*here were a variety of items one could employ to help ward off witches. **1.** *Bells,* for instance. Shopkeepers hung bells on *their doors* not to alert them to an entering customer, but to *scare off witches* . . . and other evil *spirits and demons* that might enter the store behind their patrons.

Amulets, talismans, charms, various types of *wood,* a wide variety of *stones,* sometimes *carved with symbols,* sometimes not, and other items were said to be *magical.* **2.** They were used to *ward off witchcraft* and *protect* the bearer from all sorts of *evils* and spirits. Such objects were possessions of the ancient *Christians, Egyptians, Greeks, Jews, Native Americans, Pagans, and Romans,* among others.

These protective items could be the right combination of twigs and/or herbs twisted together and hung in the doorway. Sometimes they were tied to a horse's mane or bridle, work tools, and tree branches. People also carried on their person bags stuffed with feathers, garlic, herbs, birds' feet, or any number of nasty concoctions to protect against evil magic. A mezuzah or other amulet containing written scripture, a charm, or spell might be displayed outside or inside the home or worn about the neck to help ward off witchcraft. And miniature or magical figurines of gods, goddesses, serpents, cats, boars, and other animals could be worn as jewelry or woven into the hair for protection against evil of all kinds.

19

But if t
know.....   the
desired   ....nd
accused of   evil:
"You   murdered   my child!" i

one

Magic

o work their magic, witches used their natural power along with the energy they pulled in from the Four Elements. Their talents might be so great that they could unlock doors by using only mind-thought, hurl balls of fire at their enemies, speak to animals, and see into the future.

Not every witch had the same talents, and all witches had varying levels of power. Usually, each witch had a particular specialty: she could be a great healer or seer, read the thoughts of others or have visions, or be able to summon wild beasts to her aid. Many witches befriended and protected the animals of the forest, and several witches had a familiar. A witch's familiar was a pet or animal friend to whom the witch could confide and who kept her company. It has been said from earliest times that the witch needed her familiar as an assistant in helping with witchcraft and magic. This may or may not be true. However, even the greatest goddesses had magical pets, who could cast enchantments of their own. And, whether the witch's familiar was a cat or a dog, a hare or an owl, a horse or a falcon, a squirrel or a mouse, it accompanied its mistress in almost all of her magical endeavors.

Witches lived among ordinary people as law-abiding citizens, and

22

23

caused no harm...

24

Supernatural traits and psychic ability are usually inherited, but they can sometimes be learned, as well. Often one's capacity for magic is hidden, shrugged off, or ignored. Training, study, utilization, and much hard work can bring it up to the fore. Perhaps the easiest and most important piece of advice to adhere to is this: listen to the voice within. Your intuition has much to tell you, if you would only pay attention.

Some of the most powerful witches could master all four elements: Earth, Air, Fire, and Water. But this type of power was rare. More likely, the everyday witch had one particular strength, along with a few other special talents. For example, she might possess an exceptional gift in the use and control of Air. This witch could extinguish a flame, summon a breeze, or call a great storm with the mere thought of it. A witch who had mastered the art of Fire would be able to ignite a torch, surround an army with a circle of flame, or throw fireballs by uttering a chant or spell.

After invoking these powers it was proper to acknowledge the goddess with whom the witch identified, with murmured praise and thanks, special offerings, and gratitude. Being a witch was serious business, and witches were honorable to their deities, always careful not to misuse the powers with which they had been gifted.

26

Witches could place protective wards, or charms, on themselves, their loved ones, and their homes, to keep them safe from harm or intrusion. They were sharp and intelligent, quick-witted and wise, loving and giving. They would have blended into the community as healers, weavers, or housewives; they were married and had children, valued their friends, witches or not, and attended parties. They went to local fairs, festivals, and markets. If the witch belonged to a coven, the traditional group of thirteen, she would attend celebrations of the seasons and practice magical rites with that group. If there were no coven, she would practice her religion and magical talents alone.

Witches lived among ordinary people as law-abiding citizens, and caused no harm unless relentlessly provoked. Even then, the witch would think long and hard before seeking retaliation. And, if she deemed it necessary, would strike back with not even a tenth of her power. The witches' creed today is as then: to harm none, for it would return to you threefold; likewise, a good nature would be returned in kind. It was never wise to cast cruel spells.

Witches liked to wear fine jewelry, often set with magical stones. Many of them could read and write, although they had to keep this secret. Reading and writing was uncommon among women of earlier times, even those noble born, for it was believed unnecessary. For hundreds of years, women had little or no social or political standing and anything of import was considered men's business.

Not much more than cooking and sewing, birthing babies, and tending house was expected of most women. But if a witch couldn't read and write she would have been unable to decipher written spells and magical recipes, and would have had no way of recording her own information in her Book of Shadows—a most important volume.

28

Each witch had her own Book of Shadows. As it was a type of journal or diary, no two were alike. In it she would include such things as spells, charms, and recipes; descriptions of herbs and their uses; lists of ingredients for tonics, elixirs, decoctions, and such; stories, illustrations, and current events. The witch might include a section where she kept a list of her patients, their ailments, and treatments. She may have kept records of coven meetings, holidays, rituals, and perhaps copied into her own Book information and recipes from the Books of other witches. Each witch's Book of Shadows was burned after her death. This way, she could not be accused of witchcraft and the surviving members of her family would not be subject to persecution as a result of that accusation. The Book was also burned to keep the mysteries of magic and witchcraft a secret. These days, a witch's Book may be burned, buried with her, or passed on to another family member.

A lucky witch would possess a crystal ball into which she could scry, or gaze, and see the future. However, not only were crystal balls expensive, but owning one would have marked her outright as a witch. So, more likely she would have had to use an ordinary household item, such as a pot or cauldron filled with water. Scarce and expensive during some eras, a mirror would have been ideal.

A witch may have specialized in astrology, a type of divination and prophesizing that utilized the patterns of heavenly bodies. Popularly known as "stargazing," this magical art was used for prediction and led to the modern science of astronomy.

Some witches practiced divination, or viewing the unknown. Divination has been used by all cultures throughout history, and many different objects can be used for this type of magic. The ancient Greeks used semiprecious stones placed on a red-hot ax blade, and many witches used special stones for divination, too. Sometimes the stone was disguised in the form of a beautifully handcrafted piece of jewelry.

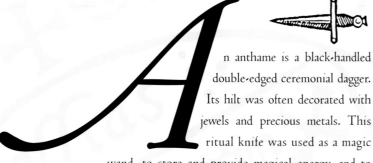

An anthame is a black-handled double-edged ceremonial dagger. Its hilt was often decorated with jewels and precious metals. This ritual knife was used as a magic wand, to store and provide magical energy, and to create, or draw, a magic circle.

A magic circle was cast to purify and create a perimeter of space wherein evil magic could not enter. Goddesses and good spirits were invited into the circle, which sometimes had powerful, protective stones placed at North, South, East, and West points. And each point was associated with one of the Four Elements. North was the most powerful direction. It represented the element of Earth, the celestial bodies revolving around the North Star, and encompassed all secrets, darkness, and the unknown.

South was the element of Fire and therefore associated with the sun. This point signified the meeting of East and West—intuition, insight, reason, and logic—and the channeling of the powers of intellect, clairvoyance, and nature. East was the direction for the element of Air, symbolizing clarity, spiritual awareness, and mysticism. West represented imagination and inspiration, as well as emotions and reason. The circle itself was a mark of infinity and eternity.

A witch would cast a magic circle by turning clockwise, beginning at East, following the revolution of the sun. The magic circle was drawn with either a magic wand or an anthame. A charm or spell was recited as the witch cast the circle, asking the presence of friendly or helpful spirits to attend. Before she closed the "gate," the witch would recite such words as "All evil stays out." And, magically, it did.

The witch welcomed any spirits that entered the magic circle, she explained why she had called them, and rituals were performed. Finally, the spirits were thanked and wished Godspeed, and the circle would be magically undone. Sometimes the magic circle was cast around one lying in sickbed or new mothers and their infants, to help keep evil spirits at bay. Candles placed around the circle signified high magic.

A magic circle was cast to purify and create a perimeter of space wherein evil magic could not enter.

32

Abracadabra is an ancient magical word that means "Hurt me not." It comes from the ancient Gnostic deity Braxus. Abracadabra might be chanted, or the letters could be worn on an inverted pyramid talisman to ensure good luck or to protect the wearer from illness or fever. It was also touted as effective relief for toothaches. Gnosticism was a cult-like Greco-Roman religion in the second century A.D. The word is derived from the Greek gnosis, meaning a person who has secret knowledge.

34

To obtain the power and secrets of witchcraft, it is necessary to visit a churchyard at midnight, and cut off the hand of a recently buried corpse with your own hand. This is preserved by drying or smoking, and can then be used with great and fatal effect.

—Lady Jane Wilde, Ancient Charms, late 1800s

But ... their skills and knowledge failed to produce th... desired results, they ... accused of evil.

" You ... dered my child!

"Witchcraft is the worship of

CELTIC WISDOM

They were the descendants of the Neolithic farmers who walked the earth four millennia ago. They were a magical, nature-oriented people who had evolved from the proto-Celts of the second millennium B.C.E. They were known for their supernatural talents. And they tossed offerings, votives, and sacrificed humans into peat bogs. They were the Celts, an unusual and curious people, indeed.

Their Druid priests practiced divination, meditation, and shape-shifting (changing from human form into another form, such as an animal or a tree), and their women were powerful prophetesses. Complex and intelligent, sometimes barbaric, often exotic, they were a tremendous society of tribes stretching across Europe, modern-day Great Britain, the British Isles, the Middle East, Asia Minor, and the Mediterranean. Evidence and artifacts of the ancient Celts have even been found in North America. Accomplished horsemen, chivalrous and fearless, the Celts regarded their women as free, independent, and wise. This was something quite unheard of by the Phoenicians, Scythians, Thracians, and other cultures of the time, most of whom treated their women as lesser possessions, lower even than the horses and sheep that grazed the land.

The Celts were very different, and all the peoples of their era knew it well. This tribal race worshiped nature, practiced magic in their daily lives, believed in reincarnation, hung on poles the embalmed heads of their enemies who had fought most valiantly—for they held that the severed heads contained and wielded great power—and honored their gods and goddesses equally. Such notables as Alexander the Great, Aristotle, Julius Caesar, and Pliny admired the Celts, and wrote of them in great, although sometimes exaggerated and rather imaginative, detail. These men, only a few among the many who did so, documented the Celts' prowess in battle, great horsemanship, barbarism, Druid priests, beautiful prophetesses, lack of political interest, and decentralized military system.

The Romans, who provided the majority of the earliest information about the Celtic people, were rather puzzled that so great a race had no interest in building a nation or amassing a great empire. But, in fact, the Celts felt no need to conquer the world. Their only rivals were the Greeks and Romans, and the Celtic people were not interested in them or their politics, other than mutual trade. But, battle they would, if the need or desire arose, in defense or for sport. True to their name, the warrior Celts (Celt means "fighter" in Gaelic), resisting surging Roman domination, were mighty enough to slaughter more than 80,000 Roman soldiers in 105 B.C.E. and seize and sack Rome in 390 B.C.E. Though Roman defense eventually drove many of them to other lands, such as Ireland, Scotland, and Wales, the Celts witnessed both the rise and fall of the Roman Empire, survived "Christianization," and their heritage and beliefs remain intact to this day.

The Celts made excellent and exquisite weapons that were the envy of all who saw them, enjoyed board games and festivals, kept bees to make honey, were master charioteers, and valued most greatly truth and honesty. They were creative artists whose ancient designs of scrollwork, spirals, and never-ending knots are still used in jewelry craft today. They are also credited with inventing the scythe and wheel plow, and were excellent weavers and metalworkers—especially skilled in ironwork—who also worked with glass and enamel. The Celts were an intelligent people who had codes of law, ruled vast territories, including Gaul and Galatia, a region encompassing modern-day Ankara, Turkey, and had distinct social classifications which included royalty, Druids, nobles, freemen, craftspeople, and peasants. They practiced a religion called Druidism, an ancient religion just as Judaism and Christianity are, although it in fact predates Christianity. Druidism was a religion of magic and mysticism, and its followers were both spiritually and intimately connected to the sacredness of nature. To the Celts, trees, rocks, streams, mountains, and rivers were sacred places, and were believed to have spirits residing within. Nature was always a part of their many rituals, and they believed that goddesses ruled over the earth, animals, and mysteries. Like the Greeks, Romans, and Egyptians they had many gods and goddesses, but above all, the Celts worshiped the mother goddess, who stood for regeneration, truth, and illumination.

An adventurous and attractive people, Celtic men were tall, handsome, and fair-haired, their tresses thickened, lightened, and slicked back with lime. Celtic women were quite lovely and statuesque, their beauty highlighted with make-up, their long wild hair smelling of earth and fresh air, flowers and herbs. All were slim and athletic, and averaged about six feet tall.

Often wealthy with livestock, valuable salt for trade, and material goods (they loved jewelry, particularly amber, bronze, gold, silver, and iron, as well as richly embroidered, colorful clothing), the Celts were an industrious and hardworking people.

Unlike many cultures of the time, they bathed often, shaved, were hospitable to travelers and traders, and wore breeches—before other peoples had discovered the idea of pants. The Celts cultivated horses, drank wine, mead, and barley beer, loved pork, frowned upon potbellies, and favored hunting boars. The wild pig was a sacred animal to the Celts, perhaps because they revered the wondrous Twrch Trwyth, a magical boar who is written of in *The Mabinogion*. Some warriors wore wild boar emblems and pig-shaped jewelry, which signified their great honor and courage in battle. Jewelry in the shapes of pigs and boars, often surrounded by knotwork or scrolls, was very popular, and they were used as powerful amulets in many other cultures as well.

The Druids and Druidesses were the mystical high priests and priestesses, magicians and wizards of the Celts. In Old Irish Gaelic, *Druí*, or Druid, means "Knowing the Oak Tree." The Oak was the most sacred tree to the Celts, and many of their rituals, ceremonies, and holidays, such as Beltane, or May Day, were held in Oak groves.

The Archdruid was the highest rank of all Druids, followed by Ovates, and then Bards. Not just religious leaders, these men and women were teachers and philosophers, judges and arbitrators, and historians and astronomers. They were lawgivers and mathematicians, geographers and healers, sorcerers and poets, magicians and shape-shifters, and renowned prophets. In fact, one Classical writer wrote of a Druidess prophesizing to Diocletian that he would be future emperor of Rome,

and of another Druidess who predicted the good fortune that would embrace the Emperor Claudius's descendants. Not only did the Druids command the great respect of their own people, but outsiders were truly in awe of these magical people, whose practices were so different from their own shamans, seers, sages, magicians, and wise men.

All celebrations and rituals were led by the Druids and were held outdoors. Among the best known of these was the cutting of the magical mistletoe. Not only was this plant thought to be a cure-all and an antidote for poisons, but also it represented the spirit and energy of the sacred Oak, and was believed to bring fertility to animals, humans, and gods and goddesses. It was common knowledge that mistletoe would keep away evil spirits and ward off black magic,

witches, and faeries. It was used to bring rain and counteract drought; and the leaves were ground and mixed with the berries into potions, draughts, and poultices for treating heart and circulatory ailments, or fused into a tea for use as a sedative or a diuretic.

No one is sure when the mistletoe cutting actually took place. Some say it was on Midsummer's Eve, as Oak is a sacred Druid tree of Midsummer, while others think it was during the solstice in December, associating it with the pagan celebration of Yule, the longest night of the year. Bonfires were lit, and Yule candles and logs were burned indoors to symbolize light in the darkest of winter and to bring inside the blessing of the sun. (The Celts originated both the Yule log and Yule candle.) And finally, some people believe it was likely cut at Samhain, when the mistletoe berries are fully ripe.

To celebrate the cutting of the thick-leaved, waxy-berried plant, first, a magnificent feast would be laid in readiness in the Oak grove of the forest. Then everyone would assemble, clothed in the best of their finery, gemstones, and jewelry, and two white bulls were led to the center of the clearing, their horns beribboned and adorned with flowers, in preparation for a sacrifice of thanks to the gods. The white-robed Druids would gather beneath the chosen Oak, the Archdruid clad in a gold-trimmed white gown. This highest priest climbed the tree, and, using a golden ceremonial sickle, cut the mistletoe and tossed it into a length of white fabric held in readiness below. The bulls were then sacrificed to gift the gods, and the celebration began. The next day, outside the home of each family hung a sprig of mistletoe as a sign of peace, goodwill, and welcome.

The demise of the Druids in all but parts of Ireland, the Scottish Highlands, and some of the unconquered British Isles began with Romanization. Battle with the Celts was fierce. Believing in a spirit life after mortal death, they had no fear of war, knowing that the next world awaited them, and they would be able to take care of any unfinished business in the Otherworld. In 60 C.E. the Welsh Druids of Mona, now Anglesey, put a curse on the advancing Roman legions. The Celtic women railed and screamed at the soldiers as the Druids cursed them, and the Roman army became so unnerved that they broke rank and had to be regrouped before attacking and decimating the defending Welsh Celts.

The Celtic people were a terrifying sight in battle. They used their lime paste to whiten and spike their hair, rode chariots and ran naked except for the golden torques they wore, and their women led the battle charge. Carrying torches and banging wooden clappers, the women blew horns and trumpets and screamed battle cries and hurled insults at the enemy, acting in honor of their war goddess Morrigna. If her man was felled in the midst of a bloodbath, it was likely that wild-haired Celtic beauty would take his place in the fighting.

The Celts also commemorated the cycles of the year. The most popular one we know is the Fire holiday Samhain, known today as Halloween. Samhain, pronounced "Sowen," was celebrated on November 1, and began on November Eve, or October 31. This was the night when summer died and winter was born. It was the beginning of the New Year, both happy and sad, a time of shape-shifting and the passing of beings to and from the Otherworld, and a night when gods and goddesses, and men and women, paired off. Samhain was a time of great magic, when the living could communicate with friends and loved ones who had passed on to the next world, and the Celts had wonderful fairs and markets to celebrate for several days. They also carved beetroots, or turnips called mangel-wurzels, into lanterns with all sorts of faces to symbolize the energy of the element of Fire and to honor the spirits of the Otherworld. From this carved, candlelit root came the American jack-o'-lantern.

The Romans left their part of the world after 400 years of domination, around 436 C.E., and the Celts lived in peace for a time. However, after the Norman Conquest in 1066, they were cut off and lived along the sidelines of the greater population. It was soon after this that they began to disappear. Scholars believe many of the Druids were murdered or forced underground to practice their ways in secret. Certainly some of them must have assimilated with the Normans; and there was still a school for Druids in Scotland until the seventeenth century. However, it was after this great disappearance that *The Mabinogion* began to be recorded. Perhaps the writing began with the "exiled" bardic Druids themselves.

Many Celtic place-names still exist in the British Isles and Great Britain, their culture and achievements have not been forgotten, and their wonderful heritage is still alive and celebrated today.

But if the
knowledge   the
desired   and
accur
" Yo

three

THE HEALING ARTS

Witches had a wealth of knowledge at their fingertips; and their forests and herb gardens were a huge pharmacy for medicinal agents. (Of course, a little magic thrown in could do small wonders, too.) The Celts, Greeks, Romans, and Egyptians used herbs as medicines as far back as 200,000 years ago, and many ancient goddesses and witches, such as Epona and Brigid, were well known as healers.

All herbs had to be dried, processed, decocted, or infused in preparation for use. When needed, they would be mixed with other agents to create an elixir, a poultice, a salve, or a potion, and sometimes they could simply be added to an everyday liquid, alcoholic or not, to make a draught. Different parts of a plant were used, depending on where its medicinal qualities lay. It might be the leaves, the flowers, or the root. Many plants, such as those of the nightshade, family, including the well-known belladonna, or deadly nightshade, were poisonous, and had to be used with the utmost care, in the tiniest doses. Toxic plants were most often used as retaliation against an enemy, and were not a part of the everyday witch's stores other than for the goodness they could provide in minute amounts for healing.

Herbs, roots, and flowers, even what many of us refer to as "weeds," were all put to good use. Peppermint could be used for stomachache, chamomile and comfrey for sores, oil of cloves for toothache, coltsfoot and cinquefoil for influenza, golden seal and marigold for wounds—the list is both vast and intriguing. There was an herbal cure for almost everything. Herbs, such as angelica, were even used to try to cure plague. To this day, the medicinal benefits of herbs, roots, and flowers are ever present in formulating drugs that can be used successfully for heart disease, ulcers, epilepsy, and more.

Despite the fact that the practice of herbal healing was frowned on by the medieval Church, almost every village and hamlet, valley and town, city and castle, had its own witch, herb wife, healer, or wise woman. Often, she was the local midwife, as well.

Herbal healing was usually passed down through the women of the family. If there was no family member to teach the craft to, another student was found. Apprentices were chosen for the skills or special talents they either inherited or simply seemed to have the knack for, or because they exhibited evidence or promise of the gift of healing or a natural, magical ability. It was common to find a seven-year-old studying with and assisting a witch or other healer, and selling her herbs at the market.

There was much to learn in becoming a skilled practitioner. Where did the agrimony grow, and what was it used for? What part of the primrose was used, and how was it prepared to make a healing ointment? What leaves needed to be dried and pounded with mortar and pestle to make a fine powder? How much henbane could be used as a painkiller and not kill the patient? Should it be a paste or oil, an infusion or decoction, a philter (a magic potion), or maybe an elixir?

Cinquefoil was an ingredient added to many witches' brews, for flying ointment and spells. It was applied as an astringent, used as a throat wash, and was helpful in treating fevers, influenza, and stomach and skin disorders. Witches kept a good supply of this herb.

Foxglove, also called witches' gloves, is a poisonous plant and the source of digitalis, a powerful stimulant used for heart ailments and blood circulation in modern medicine. Due to its toxic nature, foxglove was an herb to be used against enemies.

The ancient Druids used the yellow ray-flowered telecampagne, or elfwort, as a religious herb in their magical practices. It was also a fine treatment for coughs, colds, and congestion, and was applied as an antiseptic.

The narcotic mandrake is a powerful root that is associated with Circe and Diana. Used carefully, it functioned as an anesthetic. Love potions often included mandrake.

Wolfsbane, or monkshood, also known as aconite, is a very poisonous plant that was created and used by Hecate. Included in the recipe for flying ointment, wolfsbane was used in small careful doses to treat fevers, heart problems, rheumatism, and croup.

Wormwood, of the genus *Artemisia*, was named for Artemis, and was used to treat gangrene, ease anxiety, and relieve stomachache.

The Celts favored wood betony a cure for headache. It was also applied for rheumatism and ingested to purify blood. Betony also helped to counteract spells.

Vervain, or verbena, is a diverse herb that has many magical benefits. It was used by the Celts to ease stress, as well as by their Druid priests, who sprinkled it on their altar before ritual sweeping. Vervian helped to ward off evil and counteract spells, was worn as a fragrance by bards to gain inspiration, and was a sacred, religious herb to Diana. This herb was a treatment for congestion, anxiety, insomnia, headache, seizures, or fits, and poor eyesight. The scent of vervain was often used for love enchantment.

Herb gathering was vital among a witch's chores. If she didn't have her own herb garden or grow all that she required, a witch would go in search of her plants and roots weekly, monthly, or seasonally. Sometimes she made a special trip when she needed to stock up on a few dwindling supplies. Also, she could barter with other witches. Many herbs and flowers, barks and roots, leaves and berries would be collected for domestic as well as healing and magical use.

A young witch and her familiar—maybe a cat, a a hound, or horse—would set off, the witch's basket swinging on the crook of her arm. Carrying a packed lunch of bread, cheese, and watered wine or ale (and maybe an apple or two), she would depart at first light on a fine spring day, singing or chatting with her familiar along the way. Gathering nuts, plants, and as many of the useful herbs as she could find, she would settle by a brook or stream and share her lunch with her pet. After a rest and perhaps a refreshing swim, the young witch would start off again, finding a special this, an unexpected that, and maybe the first few sprouting somethings of the season. Soon it would be time to turn toward home, as a young woman wouldn't want to get stuck in the forest after dark. Happily she approached her cottage, her familiar by her side and a basket full of the wonderful things she had gathered. The witch had spent a long, enjoyable, and productive day in the woods. Tired now, she would feed her pet, then sup and sleep, and anticipate the morning, when she could begin working with and preparing the bounty nature had provided.

A Witch's Herb Garden

An enormous number of herbs were quite useful to the witch, and the more diverse the plant, the better. Some herbs were ingested, and others, oftentimes toxic ones, were applied externally, to wounds or sores, or rubbed into the chest to relieve congestion. Certain plants were scattered around an ailing patient's sickbed, and some herbs were used as aromatics or for flavor, to ease a bitter or unpleasant taste. Many times certain plants were grown in the herb garden simply because they smelled wonderful or were lovely to look at.

Some of these plants have more medicinal qualities than are listed below. **Use of these herbs is not advised for the layperson or novice, as many of them are poisonous.**

Agrimony ❧ Slender, spiky yellow flowers on tall stems. Used in tea for gargling to soothe the throat and ingested with honey to quiet a cough; an astringent to cleanse the skin. The leaves were used in a decoction to treat ailments of the liver.

Bay Laurel ❧ Small evergreen tree or shrub with smooth, stiff oval leaves, green- or yellow-white flowers, and purple, black, or green berries. Also called sweet bay. Leaves and berries can be toxic. Laurel leaves were not only used in cooking or to denote victory or an honor bestowed, but as an oil extract to be rubbed on bruises to promote healing, and massaged into the skin to ease sore muscles.

Coltsfoot ❧ Small yellow flowers. Large round leaves dried and heated to create a steam from which the vapors could be inhaled to ease congestion in the chest and sinus headaches. It was also an effective cough suppressant, and used to treat the flu.

Elder ❧ White fragrant blossoms, dark purple berries. Certain varieties of elder are toxic. Bark, leaves, berries, and blooms each served different purposes. The flowers could be dried and used in tea to treat colds, fevers, and influenza or infused into water for a skin astringent. Berries were dried and brewed into tea to treat stomach disorders and elder bark was dried and used to induce vomiting. The leaves were blended into an ointment to soothe and heal wounds and bruises.

Feverfew ❧ Thick stalks, daisylike flowers, large green, ragged leaves. This herb could be used in a draught or steamy bath to ease congestion and upper-respiratory ailments, as well as help regulate the menstrual cycle.

Heartsease ❧ A purplish and yellow English violet, also known as a wild pansy. Heartsease was used to treat heart ailments, respiratory problems, and sore throat. It was also used in a draught as a painkiller and as a skin ointment for rashes. This popular magical ingredient was also included in love charms.

Hellebore ❧ Yellow flowers, extremely toxic. Small amounts were applied to treat rashes, bruises, and headaches.

Lavender ❧ A leafy shrub with fragrant lavender-colored flowers. A magical herb. Large doses are toxic. Lavender water was used to cleanse skin; extracted into oil it was rubbed into the temples to treat headache and relieve pain; brewed in tea, it eased anxiety and headache, and helped to calm hysteria. Lavender was also used in pillows to promote sleep and sweet dreams.

Marshmallow ❧ Pink-flowered and broad-leaved with tall white-gray stalks, the root was the most useful part of the plant. Dried and ground, it was used as a poultice to soothe wounds, burns, and heal infection. Boiled in a liquid to which a sweetener was added, the ground root was an effective upper-respiratory decongestant.

Pennyroyal ❧ A small herb of the mint family, with scented purple or blue flowers. Can be poisonous; best used externally. Was utilized as an antiseptic for wounds and rashes, a treatment for muscle spasms and indigestion, and was mixed with vinegar and water to induce vomiting. Pennyroyal oil was an effective mosquito repellant when burned or rubbed into the skin.

Rue ❧ An unpleasant-smelling, multibranched woody herb with small, bitter leaves. Can be poisonous. Slight narcotic properties made it an effective painkiller. Rue calmed anxiety and hysteria and relieved convulsive coughing. This plant was a favorite among witches, as it was a protective herb that could be used in amulets to ward off evil and safeguard loved ones.

Wild Tansy ❧ Yellow or white flowers with feathery, bitter leaves. Extracted for use as an astringent; powdered root was ingested to expel intestinal worms. A poultice helped ease fever, anxiety, bruises, and swelling.

Wormwood ❧ Large or small yellow blooms, thick, pale green stalk, silvery-haired leaves. Poisonous. A bitter green oil was extracted from wormwood for treatment to kill intestinal parasites. It usually killed the patient too. Wormwood was also an ingredient used in the once-popular Absinthe of the 1800s.

Yarrow, or *Milfoil* ❧ Small white or pink flowers, tall stalks, fernlike leaves. Yarrow was used to stanch bleeding, heal wounds, and prevent infection; the leaves were blended with other ingredients to make an astringent ointment for skin inflammation and sores; and fresh leaves were used to brew a tea that would promote feelings of well-being.

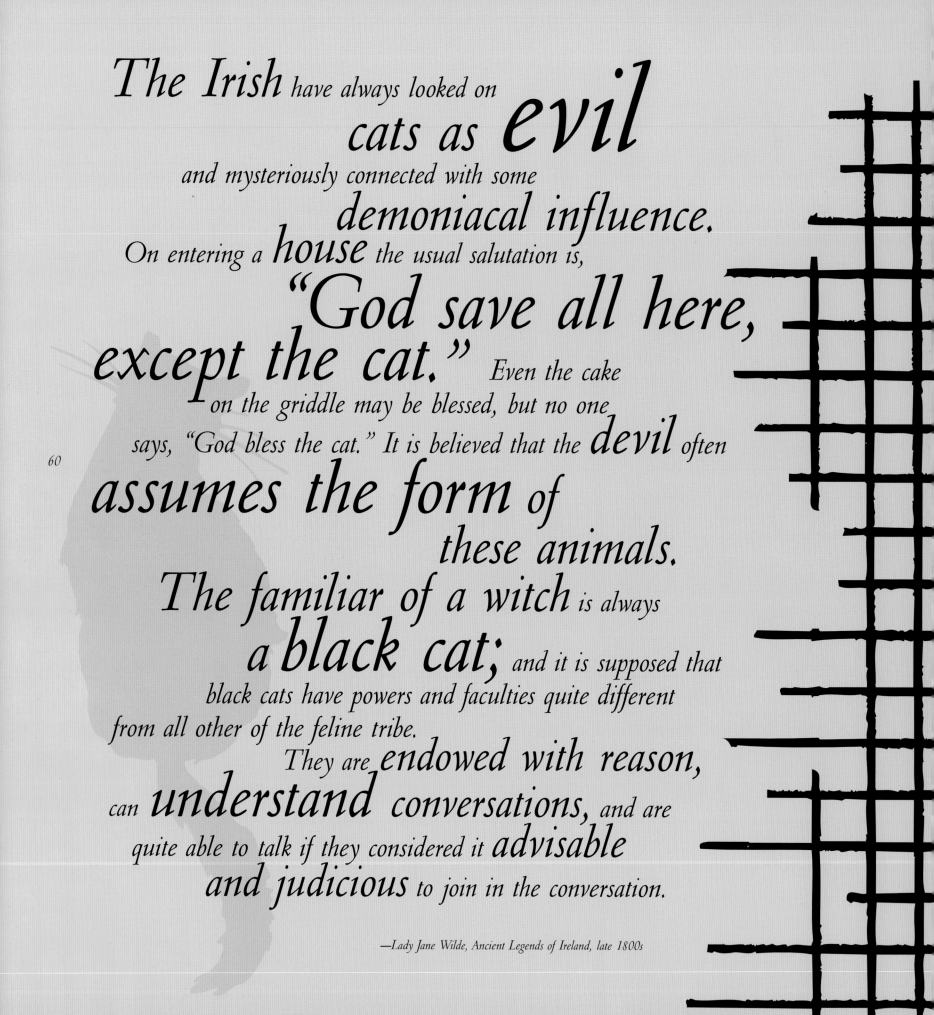

The Irish have always looked on cats as evil and mysteriously connected with some demoniacal influence. On entering a house the usual salutation is, "God save all here, except the cat." Even the cake on the griddle may be blessed, but no one says, "God bless the cat." It is believed that the devil often assumes the form of these animals. The familiar of a witch is always a black cat; and it is supposed that black cats have powers and faculties quite different from all other of the feline tribe. They are endowed with reason, can understand conversations, and are quite able to talk if they considered it advisable and judicious to join in the conversation.

—Lady Jane Wilde, Ancient Legends of Ireland, late 1800s

60

61

But if

knowled ... the

desired ... stand

accused

" You ... will!";

" Spa ... bl

at ... st week,

and ... d.";

" The

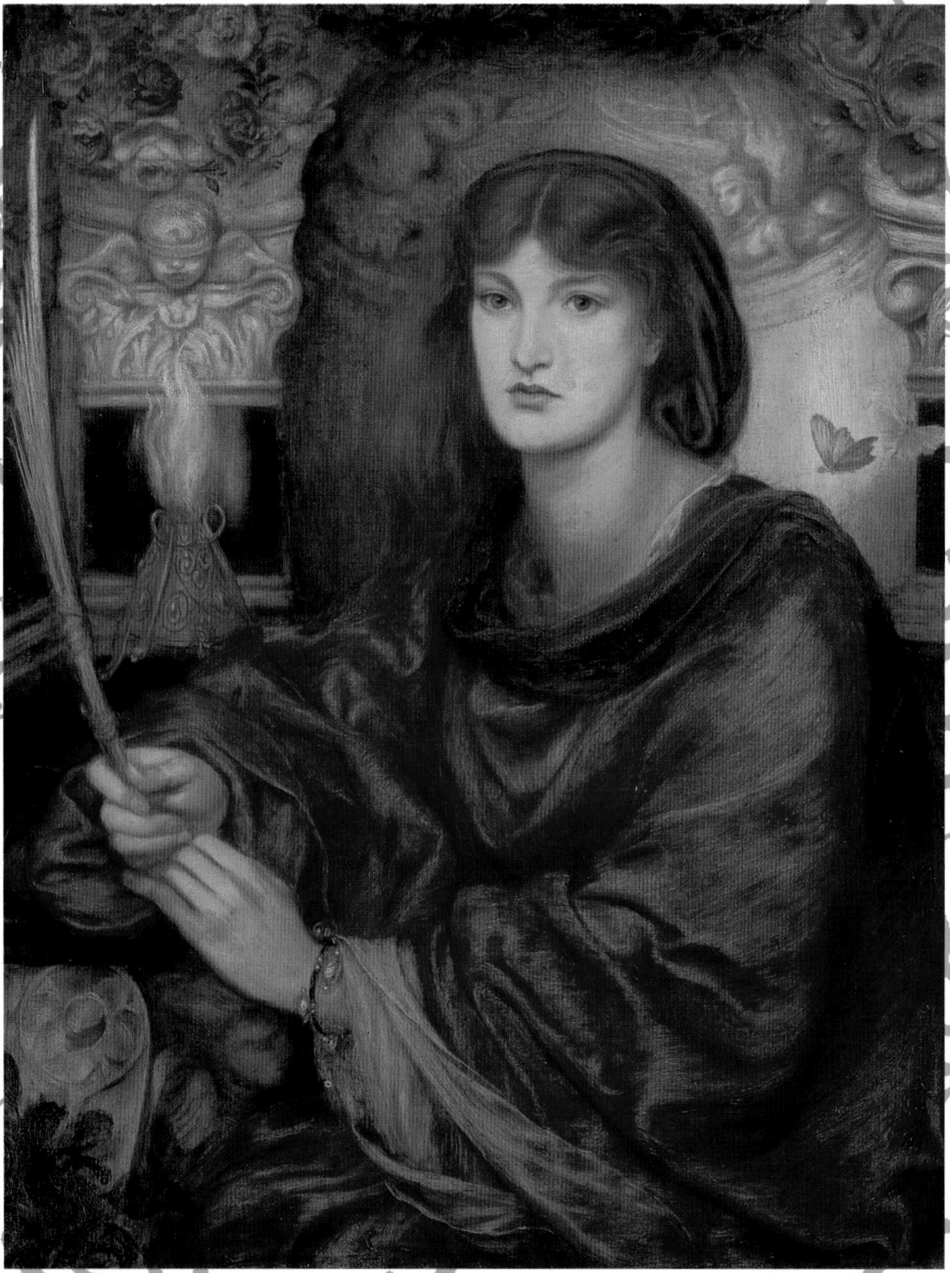

four

Wizards
and Seers

64

Sorcerers and magicians, seers and conjurers, wizards and oracles have been practicing the arts of magic, divination, prophesizing, and fortune-telling since the dawn of man. Written records going as far back as ancient Babylonia, Canaan, Egypt, and Mesopotamia indicate that there were gods and goddesses, demons and spirits, magic and mysteries to be feared or embraced even then.

The ancient Greek philosophy of magic concerned high magicians who worked through their gods and goddesses. The Egyptians were in awe of their pharaohs, whom they saw as deities possessing hereditary magical powers, and they also believed their priests worked magic through gods and goddesses as well. Hebrew sorcery involved working magic, divination, and prophesizing in a spiritual way and to enhance religious beliefs. These wizards, magicians, and sorcerers worked with and through deities as protectors and healers of their people and controllers of magical powers and energy. And people who worked magic existed in every ancient civilization that we know of.

Many centuries later, in medieval times, just about every castle, city, village, town, hamlet, or cluster of huts had its own magical person. Oftentimes they were healers as well, and all offered their advice and wisdom regarding the business of the day. Regularly consulted with on matters of the future, danger to the king or local lord, and war, these people were asked to divine or conjure visions, cast spells, and devise charms and amulets for nearly everyone. Their magical abilities were greatly respected, their opinions and advice were seriously considered, and war councils and kings engaged them in matters of great import. As healers, these people were entrusted with the health matters of royalty, nobility, and their families.

Throughout ancient history and into the Middle Ages, pilgrimages were made to speak with such people as the priestesses at Delphi; kings had on retainer magicians, wizards, and alchemists; rabbis and scholars consulted their elder sages for their wisdom and sound judgment; and whether by the nobility or the peasant, seers, magicians, and conjurers were sought out daily.

The ancient Babylonians, Canaanites, Egyptians, Greeks, Hebrews, Persians, and Romans practiced sorcery. The word sorcerer comes from many different languages, such as the Latin *sortarius,* meaning "diviner," and *sors,* meaning "spells"; and from the French *sorcier,* meaning "sorcerer" or "witch." Sorcerers and sorceresses could see into the future. They also practiced the healing arts, mixed love potions and made charms, were able to cast spells, read omens, and worked "low" magic.

"High" magic was regarded as a more powerful skill than sorcery, and wizards and magicians practiced this more advanced use of talent and power. The word wizard means "wise," from the Old English *wis* and Middle English *wysard,* and denoted a magician who was master of the highest magic. It was said the wizard wore his tall pointy hat to better communicate with the spirits, by using it as a combination megaphone and ear trumpet. His robes were decorated with maps and patterns of celestial bodies that were actually the keys to mysteries, puzzles, and ciphered magical formulas. People saw the wizard as a trustworthy man of superior wisdom, knowledge, good sense, and great magic.

The magical arts were believed to be a God-given talent. Magic, from the Persian *magos,* Latin *magia,* Greek *mageia,* and French *magique,* was a practice composed of mystical study and research, the use of otherworldly knowledge, energy, and secrets, and the art of delving into the unknown. Once viewed as a science, the origins of magic are directly related to the belief that all things exist in a natural order and all are interrelated. Magicians worked with supernatural energy to rearrange that order and create changes to their desire. The word magician comes from the Persian *magi,* or "wise men." The Magi were priests who were able to cast spells and see into the future.

Called men of "superior wisdom," magicians were able to fling open their arms and cast spells, endow themselves with long lives, murmur chants and incantations to work with mysticisms, and could place on themselves protective wards so strong that they could not be killed. They excelled at controlling and bending the elements to their

comp

will, and did occasionally use dramatic illusion, such as tossing various powders into fire to create colorful explosions of light, bedazzling their visitors with a little showmanship.

Probably the best-known wizard is Merlin the Magician of Arthurian legend. Actually a sixth-century bard named Myrddin, this wizard went mad at the battle of Ardderyd in the year 574 and lived in the Caledonian forests of Scotland as a slightly crazed and uncivilized seer and prophet. His influence as an adviser and magician was well respected and sought out nevertheless.

Seers were prophets or prophetesses who were able to foretell the inevitable. They were the most skilled at divination, or seeking the "divine will," and used the magical arts to call upon spirits and supernatural forces to show them the future. They usually used glass balls to look into the unknown, but almost any object imaginable could be, and was, used to invoke visions. Seers and seeresses could be found in every culture throughout the ancient world.

indtbeth/Kellerin von Augſpurg geburtig /
vnd betrohlich auffgeſagt vnd bekandt / daß ſie vor
gefähr 13. oder vierzehen Jahren / ſich mit dem bö
er damahlen bey einer Hochzeit in Manns-Geſtalt
n Tantz / vnd hernach in jhr Hauß kommen / der geſtalt
hen Peſt vnd Vnheil mit all
ſich g Allerh
reyfalt diſe z
dtlich Gottes

A welche nach m S
en von weniq
vnd 4. Kind
hingerichtet / vnd vmbs Leben gebracht / mit
ſie jhren leibeignen Bruder durch ein dergleichen jh
beygebrachtes Pülverlein verkrümbt / vnd
l demſelben als andern Menſchen mehr / die ein
hren Leibern Knöpffel oder ſonſten großes

Alchemists worked at trying to create or extract gold and silver from base metals, produce an elixir of immortality, and create life by artificial means. Alchemy began with the ancient Egyptians as far back as the fourth century B.C.E. The Egyptians believed that metals had magical powers, and the "chemists" who practiced this most dignified science and philosophy could be found in China, Greece, India, and Persia as well. Using the Philosopher's Stone, or lodestone, the alchemists worked through the divinities, using magical practices, symbols, charms, and visions to conduct experiments, hopeful transmutations, and other processes that never worked.

Alchemy continued to be popular throughout medieval Europe, and lodestones were used in love spells and worn as amulets and in jewelry for protection against a variety of diseases and evil magic. In fact, long ago, Julius Caesar gave his Roman soldiers lodestones to impart them with courage and protection in battle. Alchemy was a well-respected science and the seed of modern-day chemistry.

Oracles were prophets and advisers who worked as mediums through whom deities would send information and knowledge. Oracles were usually priestesses and could be found in many ancient civilizations, from Babylonia, Egypt, and Greece to Rome, Turkey, and Africa. The best-known oracles were the powerful priestesses at Greece's Shrine to Apollo, in a place called Delphi, outside of Athens.

Witch doctors exist in many tribal societies, such as those found in Africa, North America, Asia, and Australia. Throughout history, the medicine man has used healing skills, practiced magic, and protected his people against witchcraft and demons. He can still be found today in places and cultures where people believe that evil spirits and spells cause illness. Witch doctors may seek to heal by contacting helpful spirits while in a trance, donning ceremonial garb and dancing and chanting to conjure a counterspell, pounding a drum and wailing incantations to scare off evil spirits, or simply by employing healing herbs and elixirs. Some tribes had "witch-finders"—women who would go in search of the suspect spell-caster so that the evildoer could be punished or killed. Witch doctors also practice divination, using bones, seeds, and shells to see into the future.

Shamans were mystic healers and protectors who could communicate with the spirits of the Otherworld. The word shaman comes from the Siberian *saman*, or "high priest," and the Sanskrit *sramana*, meaning "one who knows." Shamans were priests or priestesses who worked magic to speak with ancestors in the spirit world, treat illnesses, and seek guidance through divination. They could be found in ancient northern Europe, Asia, and Siberia, and still exist among Native American and African peoples today.

72

For thousands of years, it was believed that every magical person had a good, or light, side, and an evil, or dark, side. People did not like to anger them for fear of the woes that might be unleashed upon them. To keep from being ensorcelled, people would wear birthstone jewelry, a Seal of Solomon or Star of David, a Cross or blessed medal, a fleur-de-lis, and any number of other amulets. They might also carry with them or have in the home, angelica, bay leaves, or holly for protection against spells, curses, demons, and witchcraft. Some people believed that evil magicians could use rumpled bedclothes to cast a spell on the person who had slept in that bed, and were quick to draw up the covers each morning. The Scots painted themselves blue with woad not just for effect, but to protect against evil magic that might be cast against them during battle. People walked around carrying bibles and wearing tallisim to ward off malevolent magic, and others would whistle or make the sign of the Cross when passing magical people.

Different spells could be deflected and counteracted in a variety of ways. Aside from magical potions, warding-off talismans, and counterspells, there were several things one could do to protect himself from harm. If, for example, the evildoer had his two magical, or sacred, fingers—the index and middle finger—extended toward you, and the words of a spell on his lips, you could raise your two fists and point them directly at the spell-caster to deflect the curse and aim it back at him. My own warding spell works well: "Bad is bad, Good is true, Whatever your evil, Thrice back at you."

73

The Italians warded off the dreaded malocchia, or "evil eye," by using an obscene gesture: placing the thumb between their first two, folded, fingers of the same hand. Others wiped out spells and curses by spitting on the ground, pointing the two magical fingers and blowing on them, or making an "X" with the two index fingers as the sign of the Cross. People would often whistle when walking past cemeteries, to ward off evil spirits; and others would wear something red for protection—a shirt, a ribbon, a kerchief, or flower—as this is a magical or lucky color all over the world.

Eventually, fear, superstition, and misguided notions put even the socially accepted wizard out of business. Soon, all of those who practiced the magical arts and sought a higher level of learning or knowledge of the unknown fell out of favor and began to be regarded with suspicion. Eventually, they, too, joined the outcast witch, who had sought safety underground.

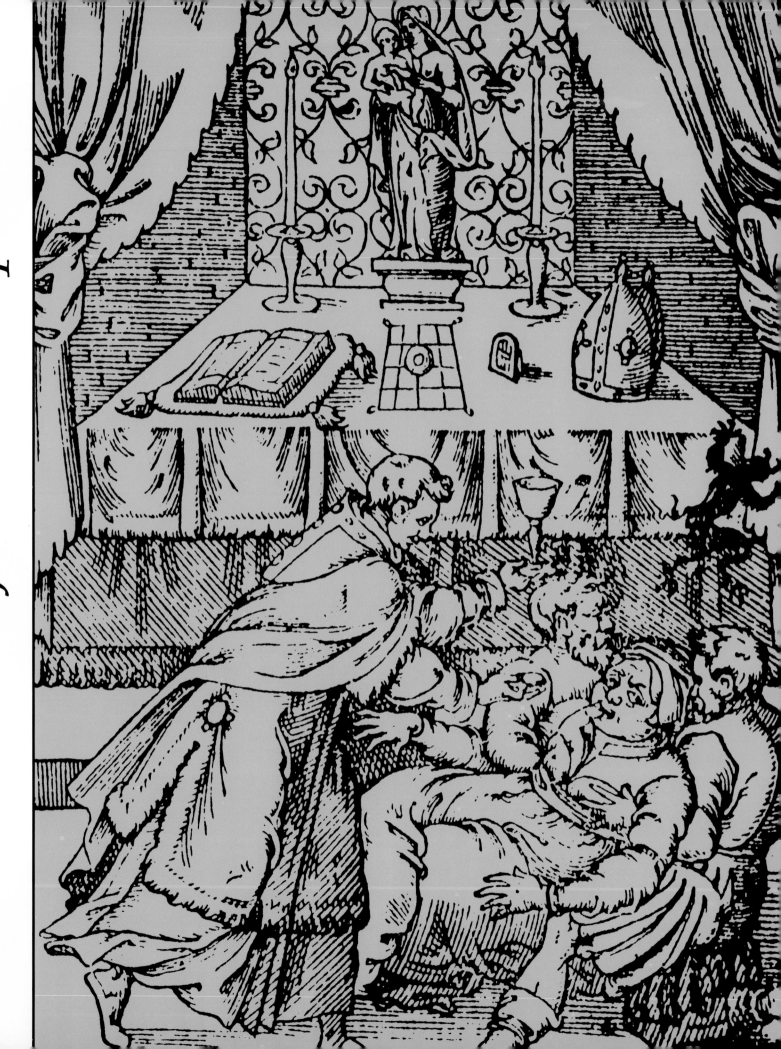

How to Tell if You're Bespelled

If you, *a friend, or a family member* had shown *signs of melancholy* *and languor and exhibited* rage and fits, *this was sufficient cause* *to suspect one was* a victim of sorcery. *Further,* *if the person suffered* loss *of appetite,* fevers, *night sweats,* achiness, and *wasting,* *these were* sure signs *of ensorcellment.* The clincher *was a marked fear* of holy people. *Of course,* *it* could've *just* *been* the flu.

Criss - cross, double cross,
Tell the monster to get lost!

—Colonial American chant to ward off evil spirits

But if

knowledge

desired

accused

" You

Spare

stand

ild ! "

lived

five

LOVE
ENCHANTMENT

82

$\mathcal{M}$oon,
moon,
tell unto me,
when
my true love
I shall see.

— To be chanted under the first full moon of the New Year

Probably the most popular reason ordinary people visited a witch was for a love potion or philter, a love charm or spell. Love magic was so in demand that it was the specialty of many witches. More often sought out by women rather than men, love potions were usually given to the intended secretly in wine, ale, mulled cider, tea, draughts, or sprinkled on food. Sometimes love powders were strewn across the desired one's clothes or pillow. Charmed items such as jewelry, fingernail or hair clippings, red fabric hearts, or ribbons were slipped into pockets, armoires, trunks, drawers, and under beds and pillows. Hopefully, for the admirer, these bewitched items would magically cause the subject of one's affection to dream of, and fall in love with, her. Oftentimes, one of the beloved's possessions was spirited away to be charmed, and then secretly returned.

Many old love potions included such ghastly things as blood, the vital organs of birds and other animals, bile, narcotics, minute amounts of poison, skin from a corpse, and other ingredients too hideous to mention.

All were dried and ground into a fine powder, mixed into a philter or left unchanged, and wrapped up in a packet. Magical incantations were spoken over the concoction, and the witch handed the potion or powder over to the ardorous young lady—often, free of charge.

Love enchantment was especially popular during the Middle Ages. However, as cultures evolved, people began to find ground hummingbird liver rather repugnant, and those of the Victorian era much preferred love charms and spells to slipping someone a gruesome mickey. In the 1800s, Lady Wilde, Oscar Wilde's mother, recommended that "Ten leaves of hemlock dried and powdered and mixed in food or drink will make the person you like love you in return." One can't help but wonder if this wouldn't have killed the subject of adoration instead!

Sometimes, more user-friendly herbs, flowers, spices, and extracts were included in love philters and powders, such as cinnamon, marigold, endive, pansy, lemon rind, iris, ginseng, basil, orange extract, vervain, mint, honey, cloves, rose petals, and coriander. These more favorable ingredients were added not only to improve aroma and taste but for their magical properties, as well.

Another ingredient occasionally tossed in love potions was the dried and ground mandrake root, which was often referred to as the "love apple." This was added to invoke passion in the reluctant heart-throb—probably due to its narcotic properties. Extract of the soporific opium poppy was used in love philters for the same reason, and hashish may have been tossed in too. Witches also included rose oil in love potions to coax the unenthusiastic beau, and sweet vervain was said to attract love simply with its fragrance. It was also believed that rubbing one's hands with oil of vervain and then touching the desired one would enchant him into returning the young woman's affections.

Sachets of lavender, rosemary, bay laurel, and thyme were either worn or placed under the pillow to attract, and help bring dreams of, one's true love. Or, the enamored young man might slip a beribboned aromatic sachet of rose petals, laurel leaves, powdered orrisroot, and allspice—along with a lock of his hair—all sprinkled with pine oil, under his sweetheart's pillow, hoping that she would dream of him. Young women bathed in scented water scattered with rose petals or rosebuds, rosemary, and powdered orrisroot in order to make themselves irresistible. Red clover, lavender, and ash leaves were worn in amulets, and periwinkle was mixed with dried, powdered worms and added to some young swain's food or drink, in order to attract love.

There are many old stories of both young women and girls venturing out at night, especially on the eve of a pagan holiday, to gather the proper herbs, scatter seeds, or toss apple peels, hoping to discover the identity of their future husband. These starry-eyed young ladies—not witches—were practicing love divination. Pulling daisy petals while chanting "He loves me, he loves me not," is a very old form of predicting the state of one's love life.

Apples were also used to foretell of true love or the status of a current sweetheart. In North America as well as Europe, girls would toss long ribbons of apple peel over their left shoulder to see the shape it landed in. The letter it most closely resembled was said to represent her intended's first initial. Other girls used apple seeds for love divination of current suitors. After slicing the apple in half, a chant was recited while counting the seeds. (See page 88.)

There were also love spells to keep beaux and spouses faithful, break up romances, and to keep lovers from leaving. Amethyst jewelry was given to keep love strong. Coriander was used to guarantee that a great love continued into the next world. And basil leaves used in cooking, rosebuds steeped in bathwater, and mistletoe hung up year-round were all said to keep the cherished from departing.

Unfortunately, sometimes the objects of love enchantment fell into the wrong hands, bewitching the spell-caster and an undesired fellow or young lady against one or the other's will. Sadly for them, the powerful charm was usually so strong that it could not be broken, and they had either to resign to their fate or suffer hopeless doom, such as a life of unrequited love, anger and faithlessness, suicide, or some other catastrophe. It was usually wiser to let nature take its course, and bring life mates together without magic or enchantment.

Note the following stories of love magic, love goddesses and sorceresses, and love enchantment gone wrong or right.

An Old Irish ballad tells the story of Allison Gross, known as "The ugliest witch i' the North Country." Allison's attempts at wooing a handsome young man were met with his unfortunate "Awa, awa, ye ugly witch." In her rage, the witch turned him into a wingless, poisonous dragon. He lived that way, twined in a tree, until a faery queen happened along and freed him from his miserable enchantment.

Caer of Ireland was a beautiful, bejeweled faery who'd been bewitched into living every other year as a swan maiden. She visited the hero Angus Og in his dreams each night for a year, and then his visions of the lovely maiden disappeared. By then, he had fallen in love with her, and searched for Caer for a year. Finally, a faery king told Angus Og the story of his beloved and where to find her. As he entered the swan maiden's lake, Angus Og was enchanted into a swan himself, and together they flew away to Tara, seat of the ancient Irish kings, where they lived happily ever after.

Queen Edain was held captive by a faery king in his crystal palace. Her husband, the king of Munster, stormed the castle with his army and a band of powerful Druids. Frightened but still unwilling to let her go, the faery king enchanted several faeries to look exactly like Edain, and her husband was unable to tell which one was actually she. By power of love, Queen Edain broke through the faery king's enchantment and ran into the arms of her adoring king. Love truly conquers all, and no magical charms are needed.

The sorceress Circe managed to bewitch her visitors into animals, but was unable to ensorcel Odysseus. The magical moly sprig given to him by the god Hermes kept Odysseus from Circe's enchantment. However, he did stay with her for a year, proving love magic unnecessary in the first place.

The Norse people had many love goddesses, the beautiful sorceress Freya first among them. She was the golden-haired, white-robed goddess of the warrior-maiden Valkyries, as well as goddess of magic, love, beauty, sexuality, and fertility. All Viking prayers of love were directed to this all-powerful mistress of the gods. Norse love goddess Lofn was summoned in prayers to bring separated lovers back together again; she did so—but only for those whom she looked upon with favor. Var, another Viking goddess of love, avenged wronged lovers when promises of marriage or other romantic matters were broken.

Long ago, an evil little faery sprite told the Celtic-Irish Prince Baile that his beloved princess-goddess Ailinn was dead. Prince Baile died of shock, and the wicked sprite gleefully ran off to tell the princess that her cherished prince was dead. Ailinn died of grief, and the two of them were buried side by side. Soon, two magical trees grew from their graves until both became entwined in an everlasting embrace. True love really does endure.

One *I love*, two *I love,* three *I love,* *I say;* Four *I love with all my heart,* Five *I* cast away. Six *he loves,* seven *she loves,* Eight *they both* love. Nine *he comes,* ten *he* tarries, Eleven *he courts,* twelve *he* marries.

—*Chant used in apple seed divination*

88

BIBLIOGRAPHY

Aghion, Irène, Claire Barbillon, and François Lissarrague. *Gods and Heroes of Classical Antiquity*. Paris: Flammarion, 1996.

Ashley, Leonard R.N. *The Complete Book of Magic and Witchcraft*. New York: Barricade Books, 1986.

——. *The Complete Book of Spells, Curses and Magical Recipes*. New York: Barricade Books, 1997.

Berk, Sally Ann. *The Naturalist's Herb Guide*. New York: Black Dog and Leventhal Publishers, 1996.

Beyerl, Paul. *The Master Book of Herbalism*. Custer, WA: Phoenix Publishing, Inc., 1984.

Buckland, Raymond. *Gypsy Love Magic*. St. Paul, MN: Llewellyn Publications, 1997.

——. Ray Buckland's *Magic Cauldron: A Potpourri of Matters Metaphysical*. St. Paul, MN: Galde Press, Inc., 1995.

Cabot, Laurie, with Jean Mills. *The Witch in Every Woman: Reawakening the Magical Nature of the Feminine to Heal, Protect, Create, and Empower*. New York: A Delta Book, Dell Publishing, 1997.

Cunningham, Scott. *The Truth About Witchcraft Today*. St. Paul, MN: Llewellyn Publications, 1997.

Dunwich, Gerina. *Wicca A to Z: A Complete Guide to the Magickal World*. Secaucus, NJ: Carol Publishing Group, 1997.

Garden, Nancy. *Witches*. New York: J.B. Lippincott Company, 1975.

Green, Miranda J. *Dictionary of Celtic Myth and Legend*. London and New York: Thames and Hudson, 1992.

Guiley, Rosemary Ellen. *The Encyclopedia of Witches and Witchcraft*. New York: Facts On File, Inc., 1989.

Heath, Jennifer. *On the Edge of Dream: The Women of Celtic Myth and Legend*. New York: Plume, Penguin Group, 1998.

Jobes, Gertrude. *Dictionary of Mythology, Folklore and Symbols*. New York: The Scarecrow Press, Inc., 1962.

King, John. *The Celtic Druids' Year*. London: Blandford, 1994.

Matthews, Caitlín and John. *The Encyclopaedia of Celtic Wisdom*. New York: Barnes & Noble Books, 1994.

McHargue, Georgess. *The Impossible People: A History of Natural and Unnatural Beings Terrible and Wonderful*. New York: Holt, Rinehart and Winston, 1972.

McLeish, Kenneth. *Myth: Myths and Legends of the World Explored*. New York: Facts On File, Inc., 1996.

Monaghan, Patricia. *The New Book of Goddesses & Heroines*. St. Paul, MN: Llewellyn Publications, 1997.

Moura, Ann. *Green Witchcraft: Folk Magic, Fairy Lore & Herb Craft*. St. Paul, MN: Llewellyn Publications, 1997.

Neugröschel, Joachim, compiled and translated by *Great Tales of Jewish Fantasy and the Occult*. Woodstock, NY: The Overlook Press, 1976, 1987

Parrinder, Geoffrey. *A Dictionary of Non-Christian Religions*. Philadelphia: The Westminster Press, 1971.

Potok, Chaim. *Wanderings*. New York: Ballantine Books, 1983.

Robbins, Rossell Hope. *The Encyclopedia of Witchcraft and Demonology*. New York: Crown Publishers, 1959.

Russell, Jeffrey B. *A History of Witchcraft: Sorcerers, Heretics and Pagans*. London and New York: Thames and Hudson, 1980.

Spence, Lewis. *The Encyclopedia of the Occult: A Compendium of Information on the Occult Sciences, Occult Personalities, Psychic Science, Magic, Spiritism and Mysticism*. London: Bracken Books, 1988.

Editors of Time-Life Books. *Witches and Witchcraft*. Alexandria, VA: Time-Life Books, 1990.

Tuitéan, Paul, and Estelle Daniels. *Pocket Guide to Wicca*. Freedom, CA: The Crossing Press, Inc., 1998.

Valiente, Doreen. *An ABC of Witchcraft, Past and Present*. Custer, WA: Phoenix Publishing, Inc., 1973.

Willis, Roy, ed. *World Mythology*. New York: Henry Holt and Company, 1993.

RESOURCES

Abyss has a free 72-page catalog featuring Witchcraft, Celtic, and New Age items, such as jewelry, music, giftware, and more. E-mail your catalog request to abyss#dist@aol.com, phone them at (413) 623-2155, or write:
Abyss
48-NWL Chester Road
Chester, MA 01011

If you're looking for magic wands, candles, ceremonial daggers, herbs, jewelry, or other magical items, *The Book of Shadows* offers a full-color catalog in print or on CD-ROM for $4 (refundable with orders over $20), or you can see their catalog on-line at book-ofshadows.cnchost.com/cat.shtml. To order either catalog, leave a message at (813) 651-9087 or send a check or money order to:
The Book of Shadows
810 Elizabeth Street
Brandon, FL 33510

Brigid's Fire offers unique, quality-crafted pagan and magical jewelry, including a large selection of earrings, charms, pins, and pendants. To order a catalog, send a check or money order for $2 to:
Brigid's Fire
P.O. Box 33912
Granada Hills, CA 91394
Or go to their Web site at http://www.adds.com/mall/brigids-fire/

Luxurious fine Celtic jewelry can be ordered from *The Celtic Lady*™ *Shop.* A little pricey, but well worth it, a wide variety of bangles, earrings, chains, and pendants are wrought or etched in Celtic knots and mazes, and include symbols of Epona, Rhiannon's magical birds, and protective or warding designs. There are magical and mythical beasts to choose from as well. You can also order rubber stamps of Celtic knots and animals, Celtic clip art, and more. Visit The Celtic Lady at www.celticlady.com to request a catalog, or write:
The Celtic Lady
California Celtic Creations
320 West Devonshire Drive
Oxnard, CA 93030

The Dragons Lair has a mail-order catalog of magic and ritual tools, such as athames, scrying mirrors, and herbs, and features jewelry, incense, parchment, Tarot cards, and books among other items. To request a catalog, phone (603) 746-6594, visit their Web site at http/www.conknet.com/~w_marchant/drglair.htm, or write to:

The Dragons Lair
1338 Hooksett Road, #113
Hooksett, NH 03106

Amazing note cards and original color and pen and ink prints of Artemis, Brigid, Cerridwen, Hecate, and Taliesin can be ordered from *Joanna Powell Colbert Artworks.* See their on-line catalog at www.nas.com/jpcolbertart, or write:
2275 LakeWhatcom, B1-1425
Bellingham, WA, 982260

Send for *Llewellyn's New Worlds of Mind & Spirit.* This 82-page book catalog/New Age magazine offers a wealth of Tarot decks and books, including just about anything and everything on Witches and Witchcraft, Wizards and Magic, Celts and Druids, and herbs and healing; they also have calendars, almanacs, nonfiction, fiction, and fantasy books. There are feature articles, recipes, book reviews, spells, horoscopes, and more. Request a copy at their Web site, www.llewellyn.com, phone (800) THE-MOON, or write to:
Llewellyn Publications
P.O. Box 64383
St. Paul, MN 55164-0383
A yearly, bimonthly subscription of six issues costs $10.

Moon Scents & Magical Blends offers a free mail-order catalog featuring herbs, teas, incense, crystals, jewelry, and ritual tools. Request a catalog by calling (800) 368-7417 or writing:
Moon Scents & Magical Blends
P.O. Box 180310
Boston, MA 02118

For a wonderful selection of elegant Celtic and magical jewelry, including bangles, earrings, pendants, and more, phone *Open Circle Distributors* at (800) 726-8032, or send a check or money order for $2 (refunded with order) to:
Open Circle Distributors
1750 East Hill Road #G
Willits, CA 95450
You can also check out their Web site at www.ancientcircles.com.

For more herbs, crystals, candles, jewelry, and books, phone *Whispered Prayers* for a catalog at (530) 894-2927, or write:
Whispered Prayers
1414 Mangrove Avenue
Chico, CA 95926

PHOTO CREDITS

COVER   *Witches' Assembly* by Frans Francken II, 1607. Photo by Erich Lessing/Art Resource.

2   Engraving by J. Aliamet after the painting *Depart pour leSabat* (Leaving for Sabbath), ca. 1650 by D. Teniers/AKG London.

6   *Two Witches Brewing up a Storm.* From *De lanijs et phitonicis mulieribus* by Ulrich Molitor/AKG London.

8   *The Four Witches.* Engraving by Albrecht Dürer, 1497.

11   *Four Heads of a Horse* by Jacques de Jhewn/Picture Collection, New York Public Library.

13   *Merlin and Nimue* by Aubrey Beardsley, 1893/94. From *Malory's Le Morte D'Arthur*/Mary Evans Picture Library.

14   *Artemis/Diana* by Arthur Rackham, 1921/Mary Evans Picture Library.

16   From *Histoire véritable de quatre lacopins*, 1549.

17   From an English pamphlet, 1589, and from Cotton Mather's Witch-hunt Pamphlet, London, 1693.

18/19   From *The Mythology of All Races, Vol III* by John Arnott MacCulloch, 1918. Bronze boar figures found at Hounslow, Middlesex, England, drown by Sheila MacCulloch.

20   *The Magic Circle* by John William Waterhouse, 1886. Tate Gallery, London, Great Britain/Art Resource.

22/23   From *The Ingoldsby Legends:* Frontispiece/Christie's Images.

24   *Lady Hamilton as Cercee* by George Romney, 1782/e.t. archive.

27   *The Weather Witches* by Hans Baldung, 1523/AKG London.

28   *The Crystal Ball* by Joseph Finnemore/The Bridgeman Art Library.

30   Early rendering of protective symbol used in ceremonial magic. The conjurer, at center, the Five Kings of the North, at top.

31   *Witches Sabbath* by Frans Francken, Victoria & Albert Museum/e.t. archive.

32   From *Collin de Plancy's Dictionnaire Infernal*, 1863/Picture Collection, New York Public Librar.,

36   Detail from Gundestrup cauldron, silver, Celtic. First century A.D./e.t. archive.

38   *Gathering the Sacred Misletoe*, Buland engraving in *L'Histoire des Papes*/Mary Evans Picture Library.

40/41   Celtic "Heavy-Headed" pin of inlaid bronze, Ireland/North Wind Picture Archives.

41   *Druids Cutting Misletoe, with Roman Soldiers*/North Wind Picture Archives.

42   *Druid Priest in Full Judicial Costume*/Picture Collection, New York Public Library.

44/45   *Druids Celebrating on New Year's Day* by R. Hope. From *Highroads of History*, 1908/Mary Evans Picture Library.

48   *The Counter-Spell by the Image* by Gaston Vuillier. Giraudon/Art Resource.

51   *The Love Potion* by Evelyn de Morgan, 1903/The Bridgeman Art Library.

52   From *De lanijs et phitonicis mulieribus* by Ulrich Molitor, Cologne, 1489.

56/57   *Witches Preparing an Ointment*, From *Wahrhaftige Zeitung. Von den Gottlosen Hexen,*1571/AKG London.

62   *Sibylla Palmifera* by Dante Gabriel Rossetti/The Bridgeman Art Library.

66/67   *Merlin diktiert Blaise seine Geschichte* (Merlin Dictates to Blaise). From *Histoire de Merlin* by Robert de Boron/AKG London.

68/69   *The Alchemist's Laboratory.* After the picture by Breughel the Elder/North Wind Picture Archives.

71   *Alexander the Great Listens to Oracle at Delphi*/e.t. archive.

72   *Dr. Johann Faust Watching a Magic Disk in His Study.* Engraving by Rembrandt van Rijn, 1652

75   *The Magician* by Edmund Dulac. From *The Wind's Tale* by Hans Christian Andersen/e.t. archive.

76   *Demon Leaving the Body of a Possessed Woman.* From *Histoires Prodigieuses* by Pierre Boaistuau, Paris, 1597.

78/79   *Dulle Griet* by David Byckaert III. Photo by Erich Lessing/Art Resource.

80   *Circe Offering the Cup to Ulysses* by John William/The Bridgeman Art Library.

84/85   Photos by Peter LaMastro.

86   *The Conversion of Ulysses* by Hippolyte-Casimir Gourse/The Bridgeman Art Library.

89   *The Fortune Teller* by Lucas van Leyden, Photo by Erich Lessing/Art Resource.

90/91   *The Fortune Teller* by Caravaggio/Nimatallah/Art Resource.

INDEX

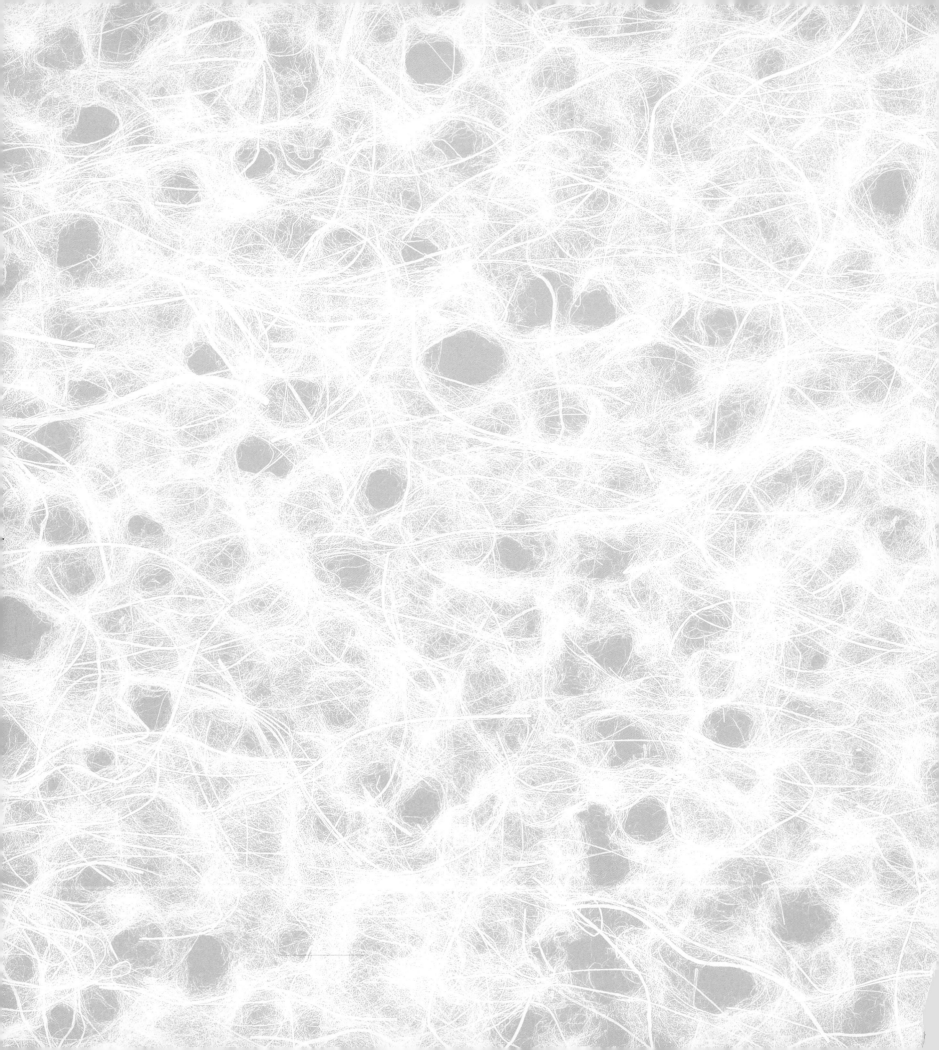